WORLD WATCH

WWF

Patricia Kendell

HODDER
Wayland

an imprint of Hodder Children's Books

WORLDWATCH SERIES
Greenpeace • WWF • Red Cross • United Nations • UNICEF • World Health Organization

Produced for Hodder Wayland by White-Thomson Publishing Ltd, 2/3 St Andrew's Place, Lewes, East Sussex BN7 1UP

 © 2003 White-Thomson Publishing

Published in Great Britain in 2003 by Hodder Wayland, an imprint of Hodder Children's Books

Project editor: Andrew Solway
Commissioning editor: Steve White-Thomson
Proofreader: Joanna Harris
Design: Jane Hawkins
Picture research: Glass Onion Pictures

British Library Cataloguing in Publication Data
Kendell, Patricia
 WWF. – (Worldwatch)
 1. World Wildlife Fund - Juvenile literature
 I. Title II. Solway, Andrew
 639.9'0601
ISBN 07502 4333 3

Printed in Hong Kong
Hodder Children's Books, a division of Hodder Headline Limited, 338 Euston Road, London NW1 3BH.

Picture acknowledgements:
Popperfoto 7, 8 (Andrew Wong), 15, 33 (Michael Steen), 40 (Viktor Korotayev), 44 (Juda Ngwenya); Still Pictures 4 (Pascal Pernot), 11, 41 (Mark Edwards), 24 (Roland Seitre), 27 top (Hartmut Schwarzbach), 35 (Mark Carward), 37 (Mike Jackson), 43 (Stephen Pern), 45 (Paul Gendell); WTPix 6, 10; WWF-UK 5 (Mike Corley), 13, 30, 31, 36, 39 (Edward Parker), 14, 16, 19, 20, 21, 27 bottom, 42 (David Lawson), 17, 18, 23 (Stuart Chapman), 22, 28, 38 (Mauri Rautkari), 32 (Mary Rae), 34 (Charles Hood).

Cover: A panda, the WWF symbol, in the wild.

Disclaimer:
The website addresses (URLs) included in this book were valid at the time of going to press. However, because of the nature of the Internet, it is possible that some addresses may have changed, or sites may have changed or closed down since publication. While the author, packager and publisher regret any inconvenience that this may cause readers, no responsibility for any such changes can be accepted by either the author, the packager or the publisher.

CONTENTS

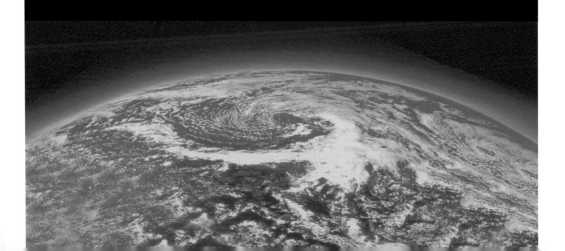

In 1959 the Spanish government had big plans to create a modern Spain. Their plans included building a giant agricultural factory on the wetlands (marshes) of the Coto Doñana, north of Cadiz. To do this, they needed to drain part of the wetlands.

A WARNING BELL

Guy Mountford was a British ornithologist who had visited the Coto Doñana several times in the 1950s. The wetlands were a wonderful place to see all kinds of birds, from flamingos and waders to the magnificent imperial eagle. But as well as their native species, the Coto Doñana wetlands were a vital pit-stop for thousands of migrating birds during their journeys from Northern Europe to Africa.

Guy Mountford realized that the plan to drain the wetland would be a disaster for migrating visitors such as the swallow, and for the many ducks and wading birds that lived there all year round. But it was too late to do anything. A part of the marshland was drained and an agricultural factory was built on the land. Pollution from the factory contaminated the River Guadalquivir, getting into the water supplies of other wetland areas.

The fate of the Coto Doñana convinced Guy Mountford, fellow naturalist Peter Scott and others that they must act. It was not only the Coto Doñana – wild places around the world were under threat from human actions. They decided to

Since 1968, the part of the Coto Doñana that WWF helped to save has been a national park. ▼

establish a fund that would raise money to help save the world's wildlife. It was the beginning of the World Wide Fund for Nature, today known as WWF.

WWF'S FIRST BIG CHALLENGE

Shortly after the founding of WWF in 1961, another large area of wetland in the Coto Doñana came up for sale. Finding a way to save this land for wildlife was WWF's first big challenge.

Guy Mountford and others from WWF began an appeal to raise money, but it wasn't enough by itself. They needed help from the Spanish government. After some long, hard discussions, General Franco, the ruler of Spain at that time, agreed to give a government grant. WWF was able to raise the rest of the money to buy the land, and the Coto Doñana was saved – for the time being.

▲ Colonies of colourful flamingos live and breed in the Coto Doñana.

A NEVER-ENDING STORY

The Coto Doñana, and places like it, continue to need WWF's support. In modern Spain, water and land are in great demand. Farmers need water to grow crops, and tourists want showers and swimming pools. The Spanish government continues to drain precious wetlands to meet these needs. So many areas have now been drained that species such as the Spanish imperial eagle and the Iberian lynx could disappear altogether.

Similar problems to these arise around the world, and there are no easy solutions. Helping people find the right balance between their needs and conserving wildlife habitats is the story of WWF.

Chapter Two:
World Wildlife Fund is Launched

WWF came into being because of the vision, energy and drive of a small number of people. One of the most important of these people was the British biologist Sir Julian Huxley. In 1948 he had also helped found a scientific conservation institution known as the International Union for Conservation of Nature (IUCN).

In December 1960, Julian Huxley went to East Africa to study wildlife in the area. He was appalled at the rapidly deteriorating state of Africa's wild animals and habitats. He wrote a series of articles for the *Observer* newspaper, warning people that the region's wildlife could disappear within the next 20 years.

The many national parks in East Africa, such as this one in Samburu, Kenya, were set up as part of the effort to combat the environmental damage that Julian Huxley described in his *Observer* articles. ▼

THE FOUNDING THREE

Julian Huxley got many letters in response to his article. One was from Victor Stolan, a German businessman living in London. He suggested that what was needed was an international organization to raise funds for conservation.

"Many parts of Africa which, fifty years ago, were swarming with game are now bare of wildlife. Cultivation is extending, native cattle are multiplying at the expense of wild animals, poaching is becoming heavier and more organized, forests are being cut down and destroyed."

Julian Huxley in the *Observer*

Julian Huxley showed this letter to his friend Max Nicholson, who was the Director General of the British Nature Conservancy. Nicholson contacted many people both in the USA and in Britain to try and interest them in Stolan's idea. One person who was immediately interested was the naturalist Peter Scott, who was at the time Vice-President of the IUCN. Another was Guy Mountford.

Scott, Nicholson and Mountford together set out a proposal for a worldwide fundraising organization to work in collaboration with existing organizations such as the IUCN. It would be called the World Wildlife Fund. Nine months after Huxley's articles appeared in the *Observer*, the World Wildlife Fund

▲ Peter Scott painting at his home in Slimbridge, England.

• •

was registered as a charity, with its headquarters in Switzerland.

THE FIRST APPEAL

Peter Scott had royal contacts, and was able to win the support of Prince Bernhard of the Netherlands, who became WWF's first president. In Britain WWF launched its first national appeal for funds in a "shock issue" of the *Daily Mirror* on 9 October 1961.

In all the *Daily Mirror* raised £50,000. National appeals followed in other countries, and within three years US $1.9 million had been raised to spend on conservation worldwide.

CHANGE AND DEVELOPMENT

In the 40 years since it was formed, WWF has often changed the focus of its work. From the beginning there were different opinions as to what WWF should be doing. For instance, at first some people thought that WWF did not take account of the needs of people in its conservation work. Peter Scott's biographer, Elspeth Huxley, believed that WWF had always understood that you can't save animals without saving their habitat, and that you can't save habitats without involving people.

However, in 1980 WWF focused more directly on human needs in its World Conservation Strategy. This argued that conservation had to meet human needs. It made the link with human development by stating that conservation could not be achieved unless plans to develop the world also helped to relieve the poverty and misery of countless millions of people.

▲ One of the issues raised in WWF's 'Caring for the Earth' document was desertification. Some areas, such as this village north of Beijing, China, have become deserts because of global warming (see pp. 38–39) and there are droughts year after year.

25th birthday celebrations

In 1986 WWF celebrated its 25th anniversary in the Italian town of Assisi with a series of events to spread the conservation message and share skills more widely. Leaders from five major world religions – Buddhism, Hinduism, Christianity, Islam and Judaism – led a pilgrimage of people from 30 countries to Assisi. At Assisi, they shared their beliefs about respecting nature.

The religious leaders took back a message to their believers all over the world – the message that conservation, like development, is about people.

Caring for the Earth

As 1990 approached, WWF faced the fact that the world had changed a great deal since it was founded. The human population had almost doubled. Deserts had spread and water reserves shrunk. Pollution of water, air and land was greater than ever. Poverty had increased and the gap between rich and poor countries had widened.

Together with the World Conservation Union (another name for the IUCN) and the United Nations Environment Programme (UNEP), WWF published 'Caring for the Earth' in 1991. This set out 132 practical actions that governments, organizations, groups and individuals could take to help conserve the environment.

The Earth Summit

In June 1992, leaders from over 150 countries met in Rio de Janeiro, Brazil, for the United Nations Conference on Environment and Development (UNCED) – better known as the 'Earth Summit'. They discussed the damaging impact of human activity on the planet and looked for solutions. Two important treaties were signed at Rio: one to regulate global warming, the other to protect biological diversity.

To the dismay of many delegates, the USA refused to sign the biodiversity treaty.

40th anniversary 2001

WWF's 40th anniversary celebrations on 7–11 September 2001 went back to where it all began – the Coto Doñana, Spain. Guido Schmidt from WWF Spain described the joy of seeing "huge flocks of migratory birds...and two imperial eagles."

At the UNCED Earth Summit in 1992 WWF activists flew over the conference in a hot air balloon carrying the slogan 'Action not hot air'. ▶

Chapter Three:
The WWF Network Today

CURRENT PRIORITIES

In order to "build a future in which humans can live in harmony with nature", WWF International has chosen six globally important issues as priorities for its work:

- forests;
- freshwater ecosystems;
- oceans and coasts;
- "flagship" species whose conservation is of special concern, such as the giant panda, polar bear, snow leopard, rhino and tiger;
- the spread of toxic (very poisonous) chemicals;
- climate change (see pp. 38–39).

The first three were chosen because they contain the richest and most varied mix of the world's life. The flagship species maintain WWF's ongoing concerns for the conservation of individual species. The last two are recognized by most of the WWF network as being particularly dangerous global threats to life on this planet. Both have serious effects on all life that are not always immediately obvious.

BUSINESS AND GOVERNMENTS

Business and governments must both become involved if environmental problems are to be resolved. WWF tries to work cooperatively with both of them to change their policies and practice. But sometimes it is important to confront them. This means spending time campaigning to change laws, to improve regulations about issues such as pollution and how resources such as timber and fish are used.

YOUNG PEOPLE

Because they are tomorrow's decision makers, WWF sees the education of young people as the key to avoiding environmental problems in the future.

This does not mean that WWF does all the education work. It is much more efficient and effective to encourage schools, colleges and

◀ Smoking heaps of untreated rubbish pollute the streets in Nairobi, Kenya. One part of WWF's mission is to encourage people to reduce the amount of waste they produce.

community groups to take on this responsibility.

In many countries, WWF has successfully persuaded the government to teach about the environment in schools and colleges.

▲ These students are doing work experience at a chemical plant in the UK on a scholarship scheme run by WWF. The students look at the environmental issues relating to the chemical industry as part of their work experience.

ORGANIZATION IN FOCUS:
WWF's Mission

This is WWF's global mission.

WWF's aim is to stop the degradation (spoiling) of the planet's natural environment and to build a future in which humans can live in harmony with nature.

It does this by working to:

• Conserve and protect life on Earth in all its many forms.

• Ensure that our use of the world's renewable natural resources (such as forests and water) is sustainable (i.e. we do not use these resources up faster than they are renewed).

• Encourage people to reduce the amount of waste they produce and cut down on all types of pollution.

Each part of the WWF network emphasizes different aspects of this mission in their work in accordance with their views and needs. For example WWF-USA places greater emphasis on conservation, while WWF UK is concerned to promote sustainable development along with conservation.

ORGANIZATION OF THE WWF NETWORK

WWF is a network organization with almost 5 million regular supporters. At the heart of the network is the International Secretariat (headquarters), based in Gland, Switzerland. It guides the overall development of WWF. The global mission statement, for instance, comes from WWF International. WWF International also coordinates campaign and fundraising activities, manages the international conservation programme and works to build global partnerships.

Working with WWF International are the national offices (NOs). They raise funds, recruit members and involve people in WWF's campaigns. Most NOs are in the rich countries of the West, but there are also offices in India, Pakistan, Malaysia and Brazil. Five NOs (the Netherlands, the USA, the UK, Switzerland and Sweden) together raise three-quarters of WWF's global income.

In addition to the NOs there are programme offices (POs). Their role is to run WWF's conservation activities in a country or region. They have no local membership and do no local fundraising. Some POs have special relationships with NOs. For example WWF Netherlands has links with the Indonesian PO and WWF UK has links with POs in African countries such as Tanzania, which were once British colonies.

This map shows the various parts of the WWF worldwide network. ▼

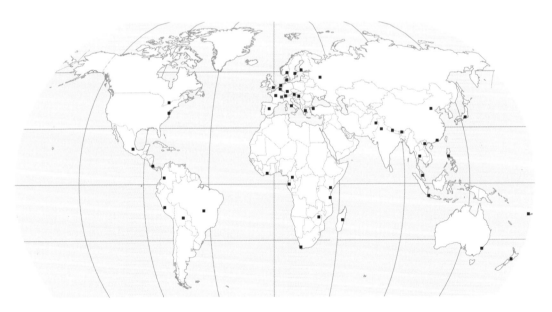

WWF Offices Worldwide
- National and Programme Offices
- International Secretariat (WWF Headquarters)
- Associate Offices (run by WWF partner organisations)

ORGANIZATION IN FOCUS:
'Greening' schools in Tanzania

In 1992 Mary 'Mama' Shuma of WWF Tanzania held her first 'greening' workshop for school inspectors and primary school teachers. One of the teachers at this workshop was Yohana Komba from Kiroka Primary School. The school used to be in a rich rainforest area, but huge numbers of trees had been used for timber and charcoal burning and the school environment was very poor.

Yohana and the children decided to try to 'green' the barren wasteland around the school by planting fruit trees and adopting simple erosion control measures. They set up compost pits and, most amazing of all, discovered how to make charcoal (an important local fuel) out of a plant called *mlenda*.

Some of the tree seedlings that the children from Kiroka School planted as part of their 'greening' project. ▼

HOW THE MONEY IS RAISED

WWF relies on its membership and the generosity of individuals for about half its funding. The panda collecting box is a familiar sight in shops and other public places.

Volunteers

WWF worldwide depends on the work of hundreds of dedicated volunteers. Volunteers around the world help to raise money through different fundraising activities. In the UK, for instance, there is a sponsored Walk for Wildlife every year. In WWF-Pakistan an annual 'spell-a-thon' is organized to raise funds. Money raised in these and other ways funds the many different national and international conservation programmes.

Government and business

Another major part of WWF income comes from government grants and from businesses. WWF has been criticized for being too dependent on governments and big companies.

Some people think that this makes it difficult for WWF to do its job properly. However, there is much to be gained from working in partnership with such powerful organizations. Companies benefit from being linked with the world's most recognizable conservation organization, while the natural world benefits from the funds raised.

More importantly, WWF works with businesses to help them move towards more sustainable ways of producing goods and using natural resources.

The Walk for Wildlife is an important fundraising event for WWF UK. Thousands of people take part in this event each year. Other WWF national offices organize similar sponsored events. ▼

▲ Prince Bernhard of the Netherlands (right) in 1981, with WWF Director-General Charles de Haes. Prince Bernhard was founding President of WWF and has been an important fundraiser for the organization.

HOW THE FUNDS ARE USED

A percentage of the money raised by individual NOs is sent to WWF International to be put into a general pot. Funds from this pot are used to support projects around the world. But each NO keeps some of the money it raises for its own projects . The Tanzanian 'Greening schools' project, for instance (see p. 13), is funded by WWF UK.

The administrative costs of WWF International come from a fund set up by Prince Bernhard in 1970. He launched an appeal that raised over US$10 million for a Nature Trust fund. WWF International uses the interest on the money to pay for its basic administration costs.

This ensures that money donated by the public to WWF International for conservation work is spent on conservation, not on administration.

Paid staff

It is essential that WWF is managed efficiently and that all donations are used effectively. In 1995, in reaction to economic recession, a fifth of the staff of WWF International was dismissed. This was a great shock to the people involved, but it saved 9 million Swiss francs each year – money that could be used for on-the-ground conservation projects.

WWF employs whatever staff are needed to achieve its mission. These could be scientists, educators, trainers or communicators. In 1973 WWF hired its first scientist, Dr Thomas E. Lovejoy. Many hundreds of scientists and professional consultants have been engaged in WWF work since then, guiding policy work and carrying it out in the field.

Chapter Four:
Saving Species

● ●

WHY SAVE SPECIES?

Saving species is not simply about caring about animals in danger of extinction – although this is important. It is about preserving the habitats on which all animals, including people, depend. We need to ensure that as many species as possible survive, because we do not know how important or useful they might be in the future. For example, if a commercial variety of a food plant such as wheat is devastated by disease, it is just possible that a variety of wheat growing in the wild would have resistance to the disease.

Unfortunately, thousands of animal and plant species are under threat. Every day, pressures such as the loss of habitat, illegal trade, overhunting, pollution and the effects of climate change (see pp. 38–39) take their toll on the world's wildlife and wildlands.

These are just some examples of the impact of these events:

- Leatherback turtles in the Pacific face extinction.
- Between the 1930s and 1980s, three subspecies of tiger disappeared.
- Giant pandas have lost half of their habitat in the past few decades.
- Despite a world ban on whaling since 1986, blue whales and northern right whales remain endangered.
- Javan and northern white rhinos are amongst the most threatened mammals on Earth.
- About an eighth of all the world's plants face extinction.

GOOD NEWS

The golden lion tamarin, a strikingly beautiful squirrel-sized animal, is found only in the lowland coastal forest in Brazil. It is critically endangered because its forest home is being cut down to make room for houses and hotels along the coast, and for rice fields and cattle pasture further inland.

● ●

◄ Golden lion tamarins get their name from the lion-like 'mane' of reddish-brown fur around their face. The coastal forest of Brazil where they live is the world's second most endangered vegetation type, after the forests of Madagascar.

There are two populations of white rhino, one in southern Africa and the other in the Democratic Republic of Congo. The northern rhinos are critically endangered: fewer than 30 of them remain, all of them in the Garamba National Park.

"whereas the time scale of evolution is very long indeed, the timescale of extinction is often short and sharp.**"**
Sir Peter Scott 1981

WWF has been involved in creating 3200 hectares of protected forest. As a result, from a low of 200 wild animals in the early 1970s, the golden lion tamarin population has recovered to its highest level in 30 years – the thousandth baby tamarin was born in the wild in 2001.

LESSONS LEARNED
WWF has been involved in saving species for over four decades. Over the years the organization has learned some of the factors that make for a successful campaign.

- Protecting forests and relocating species can sometimes be very successful, as with the golden lion tamarin.
- National Parks such as Virunga National Park in Uganda offer protection for endangered species such as the mountain gorilla. They also attract tourists, who provide a source of income for local people.

- Most importantly, any scheme must take account of the needs of local people and use their knowledge and skills.

What has been of limited success is trying to reintroduce animals bred in captivity back into their wild environment. Sadly even successful reintroductions into the wild, such as the Arabian oryx (a type of antelope), are undermined by poaching and other threats.

WWF TARGETS
By the end of this decade WWF aims to ensure that numbers of key species – the giant panda, tiger, great apes, rhinos, marine turtles and whales – are stable or increasing and that their habitats are safeguarded.

At the same time WWF will fight to stop the killing for meat, fur or other commercial purpose of at least ten of the world's most threatened animals, such as the snow leopard, sturgeon and Tibetan antelope.

In the UK, campaigns in the 1980s persuaded most people not to buy fur coats. However, in countries such as China the trade in animal furs flourishes, as this fur market shows.

THE KILLING TRADE

The worldwide illegal trade in wildlife is big business. Every year, millions of animals are killed so that their skins, teeth and bones can be turned into clothes, bags, souvenirs or traditional medicines. Millions of other wild animals are captured and sold as pets. Trees that have stood for hundreds of years are illegally logged and turned into furniture. And large numbers of plants are taken to meet the growing demand for medicines and cosmetics.

Banning the trade

WWF and IUCN run an organization called TRAFFIC (Trade Records Analysis of Flora and Fauna in Commerce). It was set up in 1976 to ensure that the trade in wild plants and animals is not a threat to the conservation of nature.

TRAFFIC has done pioneering research into the trading of key species such as tigers and rhinos. It also provides information to governments, telling them about the impact of trade on species found in their country.

WWF also works closely with CITES (Convention on International Trade in Endangered Species). This organization holds meetings every two years to get international agreement on what trade should be banned and what trade should be regulated. Currently, trade in 800 species of plants and animals is banned, and trade in a further 25,000 species is controlled. Since it was founded in 1975, none of the species protected by CITES has become extinct.

The challenge

More needs to be done to protect species in danger. There are many problems that still need to be solved.

It may be illegal to sell things made of ivory in countries such as the UK, but it is perfectly legal in, say, Zimbabwe. So elephants still get shot by poachers and the £5 billion a year trade in ivory continues.

People all over the world kill and eat animals. In some areas, animals have been hunted and eaten as 'bush meat' for generations. However, commercial hunters now come in on logging trucks and kill a huge array of wildlife, including our closest relatives the chimpanzees. The meat is then sold in big cities for high prices.

There is a strong belief in some parts of the world that medicines made from powdered rhino horn, or the bones of snow leopards and tigers, can cure all sorts of illnesses. Persuading people not to use such medicines is difficult. They have to be helped to see for themselves that using such medicine is no longer sustainable.

Last, there is the question of punishment. People caught trading wildlife illegally can be fined or imprisoned, but fines are often very small. For example, last year a UK trader caught with £350,000 worth of illegally traded items was only fined £1500. WWF UK is campaigning for tougher laws on the buying and selling of illegally traded wildlife.

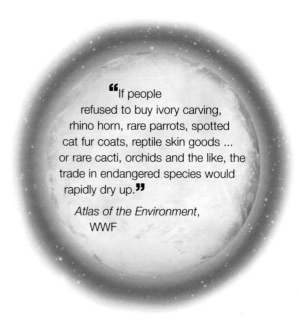

"If people refused to buy ivory carving, rhino horn, rare parrots, spotted cat fur coats, reptile skin goods ... or rare cacti, orchids and the like, the trade in endangered species would rapidly dry up."

Atlas of the Environment, WWF

UK customs officials at Birmingham International airport confiscated these carved ivory objects. ▼

▲ Siberian tigers are found in the far east of Russia. In the winter of 1995–1996 there were estimated to be 400–500 Siberian tigers, about 250 of which were cubs like this one.

"Tigers lived for hundreds of thousands of years in an ocean of forests, heavily populated with prey, where people existed in small numbers in isolated groups ... Now it is the tigers that live isolated in small numbers. An ocean of people has replaced the ocean of trees and is pressing in on the remaining islands of tiger habitat."

Peter Jackson, *Endangered Species – Tigers*

OPERATION TIGER

During the 19th and early 20th centuries, big game hunting was a perfectly acceptable pursuit. King George V of Great Britain and the Maharajah of Nepal shot 39 tigers in 11 days during a shooting party in 1911. Today hunting tigers is illegal, but the tiger is still under pressure.

Threats

Tigers are illegally hunted for their skins to make fur products, and for their bones, which are used in traditional medicines. They also have to compete with people, who cut down the forest where tigers live. As the areas where tigers can live are reduced, they come into closer contact with people. This leads to tiger attacks on livestock and sometimes on people. If this happens, the tigers are hunted down and killed.

The result of the many threats to tigers is that in the past 60 years, 3 subspecies of tiger have become extinct and the numbers of the remaining five are perilously low.

WWF launched its first conservation plan to save tigers from extinction in 1972. It provided financial support for the Indian government's Project Tiger, which aimed to set up nine dedicated tiger reserves. This was the first step in reversing the decline of the Bengal tiger.

WWF has also been involved in work to save the Amur, or Siberian tiger of eastern Russia. In the 1930s there were only 20 or 30 Siberian tigers recorded in the wild; now there are about 450.

YEAR OF THE TIGER

In the late 1990s WWF launched an international appeal for an 'emergency tiger fund'. The aim was to strengthen anti-poaching patrols across Asia, because tiger poaching remains depressingly high. As part of this appeal, WWF UK's Year of the Tiger campaign in 1998 raised more than £880,000. Another campaign by WWF-US led to a change in US law, making it illegal to sell medicines containing tiger parts.

A Bengal tiger comes to drink. About two-thirds of the 8,000 tigers that survive worldwide are Bengal tigers. ▶

FACTFILE: In *Jungle Book* country

"Slowly the elephant climbed the river bank and entered a small clearing. There, lying outstretched on the forest floor and seemingly without fear, was a tiger. Unmoved by her unexpected audience the tiger fixed her gaze on the rocks behind her. After a pause … a cub's face appeared – then two more heads popped out. Welcome to Kipling country!"

Stuart Chapman, WWF UK's head of Species Programme

Kanha National Park, where this tiger family was seen, is in the part of India where Rudyard Kipling based his *Jungle Book* stories. The area now has 17 tiger reserves, and is a focus for WWF's work to conserve tigers. The aim is to create 'corridors' of uncultivated land to connect the reserves together. This will allow tigers to move between reserves, providing them with large enough territories to find a mate and the prey they need to survive.

OPERATION PANDA

Above all animals, the giant panda is the one most associated with WWF. It is also one of the most endangered animals in the world. The dice are loaded against the panda for two main reasons. First, they are by nature very solitary animals, so they do not often mate and breed. Second, giant pandas have one main food source – bamboo – and they must eat large quantities of it to get enough nourishment to survive.

A giant panda eating bamboo. Unlike grazing animals such as cows and sheep, pandas are not adapted for getting maximum nutrition from plants. This means that a panda must eat huge amounts of bamboo to get enough nutrients. ▼

WWF's involvement in panda conservation began in 1979, when they agreed to fund a project to set up a panda breeding station at Wolong Nature Reserve in central China.

The problems

The Wolong Reserve had limited success because the underlying problems were immense.

Deforestation has been the main cause of panda losses. Between 1975 and 1985 commercial logging destroyed half the panda's habitat.

Another problem has been the dying of bamboo species. Every 30–120 years bamboo plants flower and then die. Different species flower and die at different times.

In the past, pandas have adapted to this dying back by switching the species they eat. But pandas need a large area of forest if they are to find new bamboo supplies. Because many forest areas have been cut down, both for commercial logging and to make space for China's growing population, many pandas get trapped in

"I joined WWF because I like wild animals and I am concerned that they are endangered and losing their homes ... My particular concern is for the giant panda. I did an assignment at school about them and learnt about how few pandas are left in the world. They are beautiful animals and I would not like to see them become extinct."

Benjamin Green, aged nine

small islands of forest too small to sustain them. Unable to reach fresh bamboo, they gradually starve.

Some solutions

Since 1993 WWF has helped to establish 'bamboo corridors' through farmland. These strips of forest connect together panda reserves and allow the pandas to move freely, find food and breed more easily. The goal is to bring 60 per cent of all giant panda habitat into protected areas.

Protecting the panda means protecting one of the richest temperate forests in the world. An array of amazing creatures lives there, including the golden monkey and over 200 bird species. Keeping the forests healthy also maintains the rivers that flow through them, ensuring the livelihoods of millions of people living downstream.

▲ Deng Wiejie, the head of protection on Wolong Nature reserve, dismantles a wire noose meant as a trap for a panda. Although pandas are a protected species, they are still poached for their skins.

FACTFILE: Pingwu Integrated Conservation and Development Project

Pingwu County lies in Sichuan Province and supports 230 pandas, more than any other county in China. In 1996 WWF was invited to support Wangland Nature Reserve in Pingwu. It soon became clear that the main threat to pandas lay outside the reserve. Commercial logging was destroying panda habitat at a rapid rate, but it provided more than 60 per cent of the county's revenue.

WWF and the Chinese government set up a community-based conservation project to look for alternative sources of income for local people. The exploitation of non-timber forest products such as mushrooms and honey, and ecotourism (visits to the area by tourists who are interested in wildlife) are some of the possibilities being explored.

GLOBAL 200 – BLUEPRINT FOR A LIVING PLANET

WWF's primary purpose is the conservation of the diversity of life. Although it is important that all life be conserved, WWF scientists have identified 200 large areas of the Earth that best represent the great variety of life. These may be tropical forests or large areas of freshwater wetlands, often spanning more that one country, or entire coral reef systems such as Australia's Great Barrier Reef.

Each of these large areas is known as an ecoregion. Today, much of WWF's work involves looking at the environmental problems within these ecoregions.

Population losses

WWF scientists have measured the natural wealth of the Earth's ecoregions. They have chosen certain species from forests, freshwater systems and oceans, then measured the population of each over time. Between 1970 and 1999 they found some disturbing changes:

- populations of the 319 forest species studied declined by about 12 per cent;
- populations of the 194 freshwater species studied declined by about 50 per cent;
- populations of the 217 marine species studied declined by 35 per cent.

The dry forest of Madagascar is one of the Global 200 areas. These scientists are working for WWF in Madagascar, cataloguing the plant species. ▼

FACTFILE: Ecological footprint

One way of estimating the effect of human activity on the Earth's natural resources is the 'ecological footprint'. It involves measuring the amount of food, energy and other materials that people use, and working out the area of land and sea that is needed to produce these resources, and to absorb the resulting waste.

In 1997, the ecological footprint of the global population was at least 30 per cent larger than the whole productive area of the Earth. In other words, the Earth cannot renew its natural resources fast enough to keep up with the demands of an increasing global human population.

It is possible to quibble over whether the species studied were representative ones, but the message is clear. Such large population losses tell us that all is not well in these ecoregions.

Turning the tide

But work by WWF and other environmental agencies does show that it is possible to turn the tide and reverse these depressing trends.

The story of Kemp's Ridley turtle is encouraging. The turtle nests only at a single beach in Mexico, and between 1940 and 1990 numbers dropped rapidly. People took the eggs and turtles from the beach, and turtles drowned when they got caught up in fishing nets.

Efforts to save the Kemp's Ridley turtle have involved encouraging people not to buy items made from turtle shell and using fishing techniques that do not harm the turtles. As a result, turtle numbers are gradually increasing.

However, the work of WWF and other organizations will have little effect if humans do not reduce their ecological footprint (see factfile). We can do this by cutting down on what we consume, reducing the amount of energy we use, and making less waste.

"The thin mantle of green that sustains all living organisms … is under powerful, unrelenting assault … Human beings are stretching nature's environment to the limit of her endurance.**"**

Brian E. Walker, Ex-President of the International Institute for Environment and Development

LIVING WATERS

The majority of our planet is water – yet only a very small amount of it is easily available as fresh water from rivers, lakes and springs. Water taken from these sources can be drunk, provided it is not polluted.

Giant sponges

Wetlands play a crucial role in the supply of fresh water. They act like giant sponges, absorbing rainfall then slowly releasing it into the ground. Wetlands help to purify water, and their ability to absorb sudden large increases in water helps to reduce the risk of flooding.

The demand for fresh water is very great. Access to fresh water is vital to the health and well being of people, their crops and animals. Vast numbers of plants and animals depend on wetlands around the world. We have already seen how the Coto Doñana's wetlands provide critical 'stopovers' for millions of migratory birds (see pp. 4–5).

Water wars

Concern over freshwater sources is now an international issue – some people fear that wars will be fought over water. Yet we continue to use rivers and lakes as dumping grounds, and to drain wetland areas for agriculture or building developments. Populations of freshwater plants and animals have declined by a staggering 50 per cent in the last 30 years or so.

Taking on the challenge

Many governments and industries have looked for engineering solutions to the problem of supplying fresh

FACTFILE: Salmon story

Every year salmon begin their hazardous journey from the open sea back to the cold upper river beds, where they were hatched. Here they mate and the females lay their eggs.

This journey is becoming increasingly difficult. Dams interrupt the upriver migration. Herbicides used to control weeds on farms drain off the land into the river and disrupt the salmon's sense of smell. Their chances of survival are reduced further by fishing, and by pollution of coastal waters, which affects their food sources.

The decline of species such as the wild Atlantic salmon symbolizes the bad management of Europe's rivers. It has become a focus of WWF's work to coordinate the action of communities, industry and countries to protect freshwater systems.

◀ Workers building the huge Three Gorges Dam across the Yangtze River in China. Over a million people will have to leave their homes to make room for the reservoir formed by this dam. The reservoir will cover an area rich in wildlife.

water. They have built large dams for water storage and electricity production (hydropower), and canals for carrying water to areas suffering shortages or drought.

WWF helps to monitor the work of the World Commission on Dams. WWF is broadly opposed to large dams because of the damage to wildlife caused by the flooding of large areas for reservoirs. But since dam-building is unlikely to stop, WWF encourages governments to build more environmentally friendly dams, which are smaller and include features like salmon ladders to allow salmon to get past the dam to their spawning grounds. WWF also works to find ways of bringing water to people and irrigating crops using methods that do not require large reservoirs.

The Ramsar Convention

The Convention on Wetlands, signed in Ramsar, Iran, in 1971, is an intergovernmental treaty that encourages the conservation and wise use of wetlands. About 1200 wetland sites, totalling 103 million hectares, are protected under the Ramsar Convention, but this is less than 10 per cent of the world's wetlands. Unless more is done to protect wetlands, water shortages will become more severe in at least 60 countries by the year 2050.

The giant river otter is a native of wetlands in Bolivia, South America. The Bolivian government has established three wetlands as Ramsar sites to help secure the future of the giant otter. ▶

FORESTS FOR LIFE

Forests are vital to the health of the Earth. They help control the climate and purify the air, and millions of species live in them. People rely on forests for foods, medicines, building materials and many other products. Yet still we cut them down faster than new ones can grow.

Why we should look after forests

Forests worldwide, especially rainforests, play an important part in balancing the global climate. They recycle rainfall and release moisture at a regular pace. They also draw in vast amounts of the gas carbon dioxide from the Earth's atmosphere, and give out huge amounts of oxygen. Carbon dioxide is one of the 'greenhouse gases' contributing to global warming (see pp. 38–39.)

▲ Large areas of rainforest in Brazil have been deliberately burnt down, as here, to clear the land for cattle ranching.

Forests are essential to the web of life. They are home to millions of species, Over half the world's known species of flora and fauna live in rainforests, and scientists believe that within these vast, dense forests there are many more species to be identified.

Human beings depend on forests for many products. In addition to paper and wood, forests around the world provide us with such products as oils, rubber, spices, and fruits. At least a quarter of medicines are from forests, particularly rainforests. The US National Cancer Institute has identified 3000 plants as having anti-cancer properties, and 70 per cent of them come from tropical rainforests. A drug made from the rosy periwinkle, found in the rainforests of Madagascar, saves the lives of four out of five young sufferers from leukaemia (a type of cancer).

Forest loss

Yet with so much still to discover and benefit from, almost half of the planet's original forests have disappeared. In Europe, nearly all the original forests have gone. The demand for forest products is now greater than ever before. Paper demand, for example, is expected to double in the next 50 years.

In tropical regions, unsustainable commercial logging, mining and clearing forests to raise beef cattle or grow crops have all contributed to forest loss. Atlantic forests in Brazil, home to such species as the golden lion tamarin, have been reduced to 7 per cent of their original area. Many tree species, including the much-prized big leaf mahogany, are on the verge of extinction. Short-term commercial gain always wins over long-term sustainable planning. We need to find a careful balance between the needs of people and maintaining the environment.

This map shows the world's remaining rainforests and the original forested areas. About half the world's rainforests have been lost, and much of what remains has been fragmented or degraded. ▼

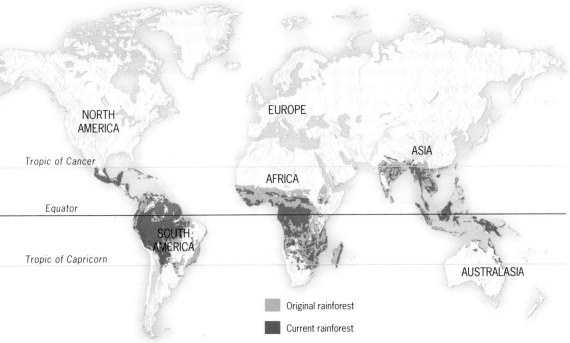

NORTH AMERICA

EUROPE

ASIA

Tropic of Cancer

AFRICA

Equator

SOUTH AMERICA

Tropic of Capricorn

AUSTRALASIA

Original rainforest

Current rainforest

Source: World Conservation Monitoring Centre

29

◄ Working with the country's large DIY chains, WWF UK has seen the FSC logo put on over 20 per cent of all wood products sold in the UK.

The idea of the FSC is that it checks the source of wood and wood products. If the wood comes from well-managed forests, where trees are not being cut down faster than new ones can grow, the FSC gives a certificate of approval. Wood and wood products with FSC approval carry the FSC logo. The promotion of this logo has been one of WWF's big achievements. Worldwide some 700 companies now belong to the FSC, and over 20,000 products carrying the FSC logo are available on the market.

TAKING ACTION TOGETHER

WWF has been working to protect forests for 40 years. There have been some successes, but still only 8 per cent of the world's remaining forests are protected, and forest landscapes continue to deteriorate.

The Forest Stewardship Council

In 1993 WWF co-founded the Forest Stewardship Council (FSC), along with other environmental and human rights organizations and 130 representatives from the timber trade. The Founding Assembly took place in Toronto, Canada. WWF provided nearly all the FSC's start-up funding.

The flooded forest

WWF UK and WWF Brazil are supporting another community project in the Amazon, which involves fruit-eating fish!

The *várzea*, or flooded forest, is one of the most important freshwater habitats in the world. In the dry season the land is punctuated by thousands of small lakes. But in the wet season, entire areas of forest are completely submerged and large numbers of fish swim through the trees.

The forest and the river are closely linked. The trees provide fruit that falls into the river and is eaten by fish. The fish in turn disperse the fruit's seeds, so more trees grow.

Now the delicate balance of the *várzea* is under threat from all sides. It has been overfished, and with fewer fish to disperse the seeds, fewer trees are growing to replace those that are cut down.

Working with local people, WWF has begun to address these problems. It has helped to plant trees along the shores, which should increase fish stocks. A community vegetable garden has been established, to give people a more varied and healthy diet, and to stop them catching and eating so many fish. Fishing has been banned in some lakes to allow fish stocks to recover while the trees mature.

This work has touched the lives of 50,000 people in the *várzea*.

Other forest projects

Globally WWF is working with many other partners to help safeguard all kinds of forests. WWF is supporting over 120 conservation projects in Latin America alone.

In Europe, WWF is working to protect the few remaining ancient forests, which are home to large carnivores – brown bears, wolves, wolverines and lynxes.

Local young people help with the tree planting in the *várzea*, Brazil. ▼

POLAR REGIONS – THE LAST WILDERNESSES

The Arctic and Antarctica are the last great wildernesses of our planet. Here scientists have unique opportunities to carry out crucial research into the state of our global well-being and the effects of climate change.

Antarctica

Antarctica's pristine wilderness is under threat because of pollution from waste left around scientific research stations, the bad effects of airstrips too close to penguin colonies, and most worrying of all, the risks of mining and drilling for oil.

The countries that signed the 1959 Antarctic Treaty recognized Antarctica as a special place that should be protected. But it took years of campaigning by WWF and others to get agreement to ban all mining and oil drilling. Finally, in 1998 the Environmental Protection Protocol came into force. This banned mining

▲ Researchers funded by WWF are tracking the movements of polar bears using radio collars. They hope this research will help us to understand how the bears will be affected by changes to the Arctic habitat.

and oil drilling in Antarctica for at least 50 years.

The Arctic

The Artic has one of the harshest environments on Earth, yet it is home to spectacular species such as polar bears, whales, seals, musk oxen, caribou and walruses. The seas are home to Atlantic salmon and plankton – very tiny animals and plants floating in the oceans that are an important food source for much ocean life.

People such as the Inuit also live here. For generations they have developed skills and understanding of their environment that are needed today to protect the Arctic.

The threats

Global warming is already upsetting the seasonal freezing and thawing of the Arctic ice. This will affect the lives of animals adapted to living there. The whole area is becoming a 'pollution sink'. Pollution drifts north, then gets locked up in the ice. Factories in the area dump toxic chemicals that are banned elsewhere. Increased oil, gas and mineral exploration disturb the wilderness.

Saving polar bears

In 1973 WWF pioneered an international agreement to protect polar bears. In association with the World Conservation Union, WWF persuaded the five Arctic nations (Canada, USA, Denmark, Norway and the USSR [now Russia]) to sign the International Agreement on the Conservation of Polar Bears and their Habitat. This agreement aimed to promote scientific study of polar bears and to control hunting. By 1983 the polar bear population had doubled to 2000. However, today the polar bear is once more in danger because of the threats noted above.

WWF'S ARCTIC PROGRAMME

In 1992 WWF International set up the Arctic Programme, based in Oslo, Norway. Since then it has worked with the eight countries whose territory lies within the Arctic Circle (the five Arctic countries plus Finland, Norway and Sweden) to protect the Arctic environment.

Oil and gas exploration and oil spills have caused damage to the fragile Arctic environment. This leaking pipeline in northern Russia is part of the problem: an estimated 15 million tonnes of crude oil leak from Russia's pipelines each year. ▼

LIVING SEAS

Oceans cover 70 per cent of the Earth's surface. They are home to millions of species that hold enormous potential as a source of food and energy. They play an essential part in the lives of human beings – 200 million people depend on fish for their livelihood. And yet the world's oceans are in a critical state.

On every ocean every day, too many boats chase too few fish. Fishermen target new fishing grounds to meet the increasing demand for fish. Populations of fish such as Atlantic salmon, sharks and swordfish are at their lowest levels in history. This is because too many of them are caught, and the young fish do not have time to grow and reproduce. Other species such as dolphins are being killed because they get caught in nets meant for fish, and drown. And all ocean life suffers because of pollution from chemicals and oil.

Less than 1 per cent of the Earth's seas are fully protected from exploitation.

Saving whales

In the past WWF has worked to protect many marine species at risk through human activity. WWF supported the 1986 moratorium (complete ban) on commercial whaling introduced by the International Whaling Commission. However, in 1992 Iceland announced that it would resume whaling.

As part of its work to protect the oceans, WWF is helping to set up and manage 100 Marine Protected Areas around the world. The largest is a marine reserve in the Galapagos, which protects such species as this sally lightfoot crab. ▼

Norway also wanted to do so and Japan has never given up whaling. Japan argues that it hunts whales for 'scientific purposes'. Since 1986 more than 21,000 whales have been killed.

WWF decided that the best way to reduce whale deaths was to campaign for a whale sanctuary in the Southern Ocean (the ocean around the Antarctic). In 1994, the Southern Ocean was declared a whale sanctuary. It links with the Indian Ocean sanctuary (established in 1979) to create the biggest protected area in the world. However, Japan does not recognize the Southern Ocean Sanctuary and continues to hunt whales there. And an attempt to create another whale sanctuary in the South Pacific was defeated at the 2002 meeting of the International Whaling Commission.

Japan estimates that there are over 760,000 minke whales like this one in the Southern Ocean – enough for them to be sustainably 'harvested'. However, other research suggests that the minke whale population is much lower. ▼

"What we are seeing is the unravelling of the food chains which make up the whole marine ecosystem. No-one knows what the long-term consequences will be – but our aim must surely be to reinstate healthy fisheries in a healthy marine ecosystem before it is too late.**"**

HRH Prince of Wales

▲ In Marovo Lagoon, in the Solomon Islands, WWF has helped set up a marine reserve where harvesting of fish is banned. After two years, the people say their reefs are healthier and fish numbers are increasing. They have renamed the area Repair Reef.

FACTFILE: Saving coral reefs

Coral reefs are the rainforests of the seas. The incredible diversity of life in a coral reef is breathtaking. But they are under threat from overfishing, pollution and the effects of climate change.

WWF-Philippines is campaigning to save the Tubbataha reef, the largest coral reef in the Philippines. The Tubbataha Reef National Marine Park protects 33,200 hectares of the Sulu Sea, which contains a diversity of sea life greater than any other area on Earth.

"It's asking a lot to close the area to fishing when communities need to fish to survive," said Romy Trono of WWF-Philippines. "But it may be the only hope we have to replenish reefs that have been overfished."

Tackling ocean pollution

The problem with the oceans is that there are no boundaries – an oil spill can drift for many kilometres affecting huge numbers of birds and other marine species. For instance, chemical waste poured into the North Sea (between the UK and Scandinavia) can be carried by currents and affect marine life far away.

WWF is pushing for a ban on the use of a chemical called tributyl tin (TBT) that is used in the paint for ship's hulls. It is known to be harmful to marine snails and oysters, and it builds up in the bodies of mammals and birds that eat the snails and oysters. WWF is working with manufacturers, dockyards and research institutions to find a less harmful alternative to TBT.

Overfishing

The Endangered Seas Campaign was launched in 1995 to help deal with the globally critical decrease in fish stocks. To do this it is working with the fishing industry as well as governments and other environmental organizations to encourage more sustainable fishing practices. One recent achievement is an agreement on fishing-free zones in the North Sea, where fish can breed in safety.

MSC – the first seafood 'eco-label'

In 1996 WWF, in partnership with the food company Unilever, formed the Marine Stewardship Council (MSC). MSC works with the fishing industry. Like the FSC (see pp. 30–31) it gives a certificate for fish caught in a way that ensures the survival of fish stocks.

The first seafood products to be given the MSC label were launched in 2000. Alaskan salmon, the New Zealand fish hoki and Western Australian rock lobster are among the products carrying the MSC label.

Overfishing of the North Sea has led to the introduction of fishing quotas, which limit the amount of fish that trawlers like this one are allowed to catch. ▶

Chapter Six:
Global Threats

● ●

CLIMATE CHANGE

We take it for granted that the weather will be broadly the same each year, with one season following another. But increasing levels of air pollution may be affecting the world's climate. Many scientists think that our planet is warming faster than at any time in the last 10,000 years.

WHAT IS THE PROBLEM?

Gases like carbon dioxide (CO_2) can trap heat. Natural levels of CO_2 in the air are very low, but they are enough to trap the Sun's heat and prevent the Earth from being a cold, lifeless rock.

Carbon dioxide in the atmosphere is essential to life, but too much CO_2 will cause the world to overheat. Humans are burning more and more coal, gas and oil for energy, which releases large amounts of CO_2 into the atmosphere. Emissions of CO_2 worldwide are now 12 times higher than they were in 1900.

Some effects of global warming:

- The Arctic sea ice has lost 14 per cent of its volume since 1978. Some scientists think that as the melting icy water flows southwards, Europe might become as cold as Northern Canada.
- People are dying in heatwaves in cities from Chicago to New Delhi.
- If sea levels rise, they could threaten low-lying islands in the Pacific and Indian Oceans.
- Super-hurricanes could well become more commonplace.
- Many scientists believe that the rapid rate of global warming puts one third of the world's forests at risk.

● ●

The effects of a drought in Naivasha, Kenya. The increased risk of droughts in this and other African countries is thought to be due to global warming. ▼

▲ Wind turbines like these in Cornwall, UK, are one way of producing energy without CO_2 emissions. But they are not a solution in themselves. It would take many thousands of wind turbines to produce even a tenth of the electricity produced using fossil fuels.

Taking action to reduce CO_2

WWF and other NGOs (non-governmental organizations like WWF) have played a big part in pressing for a reduction in CO_2 emissions following the Kyoto Protocol. The Kyoto Protocol was an agreement reached in 1997 to set targets for reducing greenhouse gas emissions.

All members of the United Nations and organizations attending the Earth Summit in Rio de Janeiro in 1992 were invited to sign the Kyoto Protocol. However, it was not until July 2001 that ministers from 178 countries finally agreed how much each country must reduce its CO_2 emissions.

How de we reduce CO_2?

Cutting CO_2 emissions involves saving energy and looking for alternative ways of producing electricity (for instance using wind or solar power). WWF is urging the developed, industrialized countries to reduce their CO_2 emissions to 10 per cent below their 1990 levels in the next 10 years.

But even if these targets are achieved, the amount of CO_2 in the atmosphere will continue to rise. The UN estimates that it would take at least a 60 per cent reduction in CO_2 to stabilize concentrations in the atmosphere at their present level, and such a reduction is impossible.

TOXIC CHEMICALS

Modern society has developed a huge array of synthetic chemicals to control disease, increase food production, and kill pests. Our daily lives are now much easier than in the past, but there is a big question mark about the long-term effects of some of these chemicals on people and the environment. Research in this area is now a high priority for WWF.

POPs

Most worrying are those chemicals described as persistent organic pollutants or POPs. These are dangerous because besides being toxic (poisonous), they do not break down easily and they collect in body fat. Most importantly POPs can travel thousands of miles. One country's contamination becomes the world's problem.

Urgent action is required to deal with POPs.

Some effects

People and animals around the world are developing a range of medical conditions and sexual abnormalities

▲ These factories at Nuzhny Tagil in Russia were until recently releasing large quantities of chemicals into the air. However, in the last three or four years the factories have reduced the amount of pollution they produce by two-thirds.

that scientists believe are directly linked to chemical pollution:

- Beluga whales in the St Lawrence River (between the USA and Canada) suffer from an astonishing list of disorders that are not seen in whales from other waters. One reason might be pollution from the huge number of ships that travel along the river.
- In the late 1980s and early 1990s thousands of seals, dolphins and porpoises suddenly died. This is thought to have been an indirect effect of pollutants such as DDT, a chemical that was used as an insecticide until it was found to have harmful effects.
- Scientific studies of large predators such as polar bears show they have high levels of chemicals called PCBs

(polychlorinated biphenyls) in their body fat. PCBs are used in plastics and many other products. Even very small doses can cause harm to young or unborn animals.

- Worryingly high levels of PCBs have been found in the breast milk of Inuit women in the Arctic. These women live thousands of kilometres from the nearest source of PCBs, showing just how far toxic chemicals can travel.

Global breakthrough

WWF played an important part in negotiations started in 1997 that were aimed at reducing the dangers of POPs. In 2000, 122 countries signed a major global agreement, the Stockholm Convention, which called for the global elimination of POPs.

However, this agreement does not solve the problem by itself. It needs the full support of governments, industry and consumers if it is to reach its goal of reducing the production and use of toxic chemicals.

FACTFILE: Silent Spring

Rachel Carson wrote the book *Silent Spring* in 1962 to warn the world of the dangers of using synthetic pesticides on food crops. In 1944 scientists found residues of the pesticide DDT in human fat. Seven years later there was disturbing news of DDT contaminating the milk of nursing mothers. In the early 1950s naturalists saw the effects of pesticides on wildlife, such as the thinning of bird eggshells.

Pesticides being sprayed on fruit trees in Po River valley, Italy. It is best to thoroughly wash fruit that is not organic, to get rid of any pesticide residues on the skin. ▼

POVERTY AND DEVELOPMENT

Many people still think of WWF as an organization that saves furry animals. But as we have seen, WWF is about much more. It has long believed that you cannot get rid of poverty without protecting the environment and you cannot protect the environment without tackling poverty.

Today WWF spends half of its conservation funds on helping people to find ways to live and work that do not damage their environment. This is known as sustainable development. By promoting sustainable development throughout the world, WWF aims to ensure that the benefits and wonders of nature will still be there for future generations.

People and the planet

Some of the poorest people in the world live in the most fragile environments. WWF is working with some of the world's poorest people – helping them to help themselves by

▲ The snow leopard is one of WWF's flagship species.

finding practical ways in which they can earn a living with minimal damage to their natural environment. WWF UK has run a campaign called People and the Planet in collaboration with other parts of the WWF network, governments and other local agencies. The countries that have been targeted are Namibia, Colombia, the Solomon Islands, Tanzania and Brazil.

The Irbis Enterprise

The nomads and herders of Mongolia's Altai Mountains share their home with some 700 snow leopards. Snow leopards are one of WWF's flagship species (see p. 10) and much work is being done to help these people live in harmony with snow leopards.

The people of the Altai Mountains herd camels, goats and sheep, selling the wool and hides to passing traders.

But economic pressures and a growing population have caused them to increase their herds.

As the herds increase, wild sheep and goats – the snow leopard's prey – are being squeezed out of their habitat. This has meant less food for the snow leopards, which have begun to attack the herders' animals.

The traditional solution to this problem would have been to separate the people and wildlife through the creation of protected areas such as national parks. But in Mongolia WWF has taken a different approach. It is supporting the Irbis Enterprise, a project that helps herders to make

and sell products from the wool and hide of their animals. So instead of selling a kilogram of camel wool for around US$1, they can make four hats from the wool and sell them for US$4 each.

Irbis helps the herders with the marketing and distribution of their products. In return the herders sign a contract agreeing to use herding practices that will not harm snow leopards or their prey.

"The challenge the world faces is to manage the environment in a way that both conserves resources and gives higher incomes to the poor. We cannot care for the planet without caring better for its people.**"**

Clare Short, UK Secretary of State for International Development, 2001

A herd girl rounding up sheep in the Tul Valley in Mongolia. Conflict between the needs of herders and the lives of the snow leopards in the Altai Mountains led to WWF's involvement in the Irbis Project. ▼

Since its foundation in 1961, WWF has had to adapt and change to meet new challenges. It has grown from modest beginnings into a global organization that can talk to decision-makers and political leaders. But though WWF can make its voice heard, leaders sometimes ignore what it has to say.

JOHANNESBURG SUMMIT

We saw earlier (pp. 24–25) that people are using up more of the Earth's resources than they put back. The key to the future of the planet is to change this and live sustainably, i.e. in such a way that we use no more energy and produce no more waste than the Earth can deal with through natural processes.

In 2002 over 100 world leaders met in Johannesburg, ten years after the Earth Summit in Rio, to discuss ways of making the world fairer and development more sustainable.

The WWF focus for the conference was on poverty. Its main targets were:

- to provide 10 per cent of energy from renewable sources by 2010, and agree a world plan for clean, affordable energy by 2015;
- to cut by half the number of people without safe drinking water and proper sanitation by 2015;
- to close the widening gap between rich and poor countries;
- to use more sustainable products and processes for the items we consume;
- to restore and look after ecosystems worldwide.

In the event, few of these targets were met. World leaders agreed on the goal for drinking water and sanitation, but no agreement was reached on delivering energy to the

◀ Children sing in front of an inflatable Earth at the opening ceremony of the World Summit on Sustainable Development, Johannesburg, South Africa. The Summit had worthy aims, but there was little agreement on action.

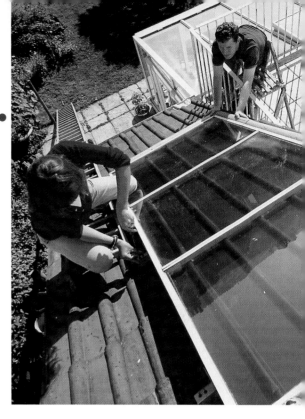

2 billion people who have no access to energy services.

The Johannesburg Summit also saw a move towards voluntary action rather than action by governments. The message was clear. If we want a sustainable world, the choices we make as individuals are more important than ever before.

TAKING ACTION

We can all make small changes in our lifestyles that will ensure a future for our children's children:

- We have great power as consumers. If we say we do not want food containing harmful chemicals, for instance, businesses have to listen. Similarly we can choose to buy goods traded fairly and produced sustainably.

▲ Fitting a solar panel to the roof of a house. Solar panels can either generate electricity or heat water. This can reduce our use of fossil fuels.

- We can do lots of small things to save energy, such as not leaving the TV on standby and only putting as much water as we need in the kettle. Added up, small changes can save huge amounts of energy.
- Walking, cycling or taking public transport whenever possible helps to reduce pollution caused by cars.
- Recycling is now common, but it is more important to try and buy fewer products. Repair broken items, reuse old things or pass them on to people who can use them.

WWF can only fulfil its mission with help from people like us.

"Sustainable development will not happen of its own accord. It will happen because individuals and groups band together, in the name of all humankind, to give the idea a decisive push."

Kofi Annan, Secretary General of the UN

biodiversity the many different forms of life.

bush meat wild animals traditionally killed for food in developing countries.

campaign a series of events organized to get across a point or produce a change.

carnivore a meat-eating animal or plant.

climate change when something happens to the climate that is significantly different from what is expected, such as the Earth getting warmer.

colony a large group of animals living together, or a country ruled by a more powerful country.

conservation preserving nature so that it can continue in a healthy state.

consumer a user of the Earth's resources and the products made from them.

contamination when something becomes polluted or poisonous.

cultivation making plants grow: farming.

deforestation the loss of trees from a forest by natural or human action.

degradation something getting worse.

delegate a representative; someone given the power to act on the behalf of others.

ecoregions large areas of the Earth that have similar conditions, such as tropical rainforests, deserts or coral reefs.

ecosystem a group of plants and animals that live together in a particular place.

endangered an animal or plant that is in great danger of becoming extinct.

evolution the process of change from simple to complex life forms over long periods of time.

exploitation taking too much of a natural resource such as timber or fish.

extinction when a particular plant or animal species dies out completely.

habitat the environment in which an animal or plant lives.

herbicide a chemical that kills specific plants (usually those that compete with a crop plant).

irrigation bringing water to where it is needed to grow crops.

lobby try to persuade people in power of your point of view, usually by writing or talking to them.

migration moving from one place to another (e.g. the salmon migrates each year from the sea to the river where it was born to mate and lays its eggs).

minerals natural substances that are neither plant nor animal.

natural resources anything found in or on the Earth that was not made or put there by human beings.

organic pollutants pollutants that are organic chemicals (chemicals made mainly from carbon and hydrogen).

ornithologist someone who studies birds and their habitats.

pesticide a chemical used to kill specific animals (often insect pests).

poaching illegal hunting.

predator an animal that hunts another animal for food.

prey an animal that is hunted by another animal for food.

revenue the income of a person or government.

sanitation providing healthy living

species a group of plants or animals with similar characteristics that can breed together.

subspecies a group within a species with some different characteristics to the rest of the species.

sustainable something that can continue happening into the future.

temperate forest forest growing in a temperate climate (where there are warm summers and mild winters).

wetland land that absorbs and holds water, such as a floodplain or marsh.

zoologist someone who studies animals and their habitats.

FURTHER READING

World Organizations: World Wildlife Fund, Jillian Powell, Franklin Watts, 2001

21st Century Debates: Waste, Recycling, Reuse, Rob Bowden, Hodder Wayland, 2001

21st Century Debates: Energy, Ewan McLeish, Hodder Wayland, 2001

21st Century Debates: Climate Change, Simon Scoones, Hodder Wayland, 2001

Rescue Mission 2002, Peacechild International, 2002. This is an assessment of how far we have come from the Earth Summit in Rio through the eyes of young people around the world.

Pachamama: Our Earth, Our Future, Peacechild International, 2001. Young people from over 70 countries produced this introduction to environmental issues.

WEBSITES

http://www.panda.org
The website for WWF International, with links to WWF national offices. There is a 'Virtual Wildlife' section for kids and fact sheets on a range of issues for more able readers.

USEFUL ADDRESSES
WWF-International
Avenue du Mont-Blanc
CH-1196 Gland
Switzerland
Tel: 0041 22 364 9111/8836

WWF UK
Panda House, Weyside Park
Godalming, Surrey GU7 1XR
Tel: 01483 426444